The Washington Poems

by

C. P. Klapper

Abstract Development, LLC
Edison, NJ

First Edition, 1985, Unpublished Copyrighted.

Second Edition, 2005, eBook. "Duet" revised.

Third Edition, 2008, Paperback. "Duet" revised.

ISBN-13: 978-1-934882-00-9 (paperback)

Library of Congress Control Number: 2008900774

Printed in the United States of America.

Dedication

To God
from whom all blessings flow
I dedicate here
the firstfruits of my pen

Introduction

A Washington year is four
each but a season
the hope of spring
the toilsome heat of summer
before the autumn harvest of truth
brings the wisdom of winter

Each season but an hour
in a watch over the Republic
seeing neither coming nor going
not noting this poet
Why should it
record each visit

There are times
which only we can mark
for history misses
the offbeat remark or rhyme
between the pulses of power

So before it pass from remembrance
into the oblivion of the forgotten
I grasp the fleeting presence of that past
the shadows in the verses I have written

Summer

The Washington Poems

Heat

Heat hot
Sweat not
sweet
By early week
Already reek
Two eyes
between thighs
Ruined four
Bolster more
Washing tons
Easy puns
Easy go
Money owe

The Washington Poems

Candidate

Fame undeserving
From silliness unswerving
Man of the hour
considering more power
a church attending
His saintliness mending
Replies to the press
This nation's mass mess
But will he or not
What it takes has he got
Too early to run
Let another jump the gun
By being so coy
He editors will annoy
Yet the papers say
Soon will he join the fray

The Washington Poems

The Night Sky

Twinkle, twinkle little star
I think I'll hang out in a bar.

Twinkle, twinkle beer in glass
I wonder who's the comely lass?

Twinkle, twinkle dancing eyes
I wonder if she knows they're lies?

Twinkle, twinkle little feet
right up to my three-room suite.

The Washington Poems

White Town

Light
Light upon an empty Stage
Life?
Life does not here its battles wage

All are dispersed by gloom of light
the marble's glorious white
is a leprosy of the soul

Mountain Paradise

A paradise she is
the summit her face
atop her tempting contours
Mounting up the graceful lines
of her neck
hungering, but only licking the face
of the cliff
who falls is lost
in the numb pleasure
in nothingness in her

Still I climb to the crest
I rise and see
the wide pool of her eyes
invite me to dive
and sink in her beauty
Ah!

To drink, to drown
At the water's edge
delicately lined by
the high-arching sky
of her brow
And by the wide stem
billowing to twin cups

tenderly flaring in tandem
a wild beat behind the veil
passion pulsing through the sheer
Below those throbbing bulbs
drops, now, a fruit
more exotic, more ripe
than man may calmly taste
swollen with captive sweetness
one does not eat
but drink those lips
sucking its juices slowly into the soul
lest in biting her nectar drips
down her soft, firm
nymphean form
undrunk upon the ground

0! A paradise is that face
I gaze for a day and day and day and
never know a day to pass

The Washington Poems

The Despair Unruly

Oft in the struggles of our land
there comes a despair unruly
Fueled by the fire of prospects denied
that seeks not now to renew the fight
but the hopes of others defy

Do not, do not, but do not help
we will not, will not work with you
but tie you in the nots of rules
lest any service you might do

So proud they reign over dormant lives
protecting years of waste
Telling voters horrors, lies
to still the cry for haste

While lapping up their special wage
a bowl of milk and plums
The fat crats wait for pension age
to leave their work undone

The Washington Poems

Sadat

How can words express the senseless
Or reason explain the work of madness
Our minds stutter on an inutterable horror
The city hushes at the thought: They shot Sadat

In a slaughter more than savage
Felled by a weapon too brutal for flesh

Is this always to be the fate of the man
who dares to live for peace
To be killed for it as well
by the cowardly minions of mayhem

Why? What cause could be more precious than
a life well spent, the world sighs
How silly become the squabbles of men
when the bravest and the purest die

Duet

Even before your face I knew
I thought 'twas mine to woo
Never mind that others see it
wish it theirs alone to view

Just as the village clock is midday seen of all
who are struck by that beauty upon the tower tall

For when its face reads one, it means it
Never mind who sees
for ringing by a stroke within it
sweetly rung for you

And as
just as
that one bell chimes for one
and not for five or four or three or two

My heart beats love
my heart beats
only for you
my heart beats
only for you
my heart beats only, only for you

And as our day shines on
My hands spread wide to welcome you

My heart beats race as we embrace
My doubling chimes ring out
a joyous concert of our love
and ever as they ring
our hearts together sing
of my love for you
each stroke beats true
our souls and bodies share the tune

each heartbeat love
each heartbeat love
Each happy heartbeat of our love.

And at the end, our hands clasp tight
our trembling walk into the night
into the night

where my heart beats
my heart beats
only for you
my heart beats
only for you
my heart beats only, only for you
my heart beats love
only for you
my heart beats love
only for you
for
you

The Washington Poems

The Library

Astride the wind-soaked city
a giant palace stands
with proportions for the Titans
upon a wearied land.

Men are too weak to approach
or if they enter, swiftly leave
like flies succumbing to a gentle breeze.

Will smaller buildings ever house
the works of little men
lest large size scatter them
when they dare to work again
or sweeping rays from salt-white pillars
find all fleeing of their lot
from brilliance outshining the sun?

Within
the babble of old thought enshrined
needs new stone to replace the rot.
It's not.
It is humbled to death
crushed to its silence underground.

Can, then, this huge hollow hall
this voiceless void for man and his echo
this shell be sound?

The Washington Poems

Heartbroke

I have summoned already
my heart to expire
to kindle no more
the romantic fire:

Die, heart, die!
Before you kill me
The tow lines you throw
are to a sinking hope.

Quick! Cut the cord
and excise passion.
I cannot feel without pain,
so is better not to feel at all,
letting passion sink into
the seasons of the past.

Leave a loveless mind
free to think without a fancy.
For if once I tried to love anew
I would throw my heart
at that old and distant
unforgotten hope
and drown in despair.

The People

The people of this land
their only tie a place
which could be here as there
The people of this land could be
The people of that land as well

Demagogues call them
The people of this nation
which is to say
not people at all
but a will
Nor yet a thought
but a whim
And helpless are those who would still the tide
of opinion made king

The people say...
The people want...
The people need...
This and that
with one voice
to the ear of the politician
loud, swaggering, deaf

But no!
The people talk with many voices
diverse and contradictory.
If contrary thoughts are treason
then people are treason, too.
How is it the will of the people
if all lockstep march
their minds locked
their feet stepping by another will?
The popular will stilling
The unpopular freedom to think
all find precious when they lack it later.

But this people make agreement to act as one
on the basis of a vote
with restrictions to protect their personhood.
Without these limits
these assurances of freedom
it would be useless to concert.
There would be no people
to gain the gain
from their concerted act.

The Washington Poems

Weekend

The weekend of my demise
a holiday of lies
of feigned joy
and captive release

Amidst the admitted troubles
of the week
is the prize I seek
yet never won
when week is done
to begin the weekend of my demise

Autumn

The Washington Poems

A Park at Night

Sentinels still and silent
Benchmarks of the calm
In night's clear shadow-light
A stage without a play

Wind wraps her arms around you
So sweet, so soft, so warm
She strokes your hair and whispers
in the years before the morn

The Washington Poems

Deacon

From prophets and from holy men
we yearn to see a vision
of life and hope
burning in the desert air
But from this deacon all we heard
was a litany of horrors
and a creed of despair

The Washington Poems

Bitter

Dreams are bitter upon us
and end as our wake
The tossing flowers
bloom as death
Their smell our ache
Dreams are bitter upon us
but bitterer, bitterer as we wake.

The Washington Poems

Home in the Rose Garden

O give Jimmy a home
Where Teddy won't roam
Where the polls show calamity pays
Where the kooks in Iran
Can give Jimmy more fans
To vote for him primary day

Home, home in the Rose Garden
Where an incumbent president can play
Where seldom is heard
A discouraging word
Though the future is cloudier each day

A Play

Does it storm sir?
Fast and furious
Nay it is still
If it still storms
I am still right
Nay it stopped
How is it fast and furious?
Its fury has been fast
raining in my neck of woods
in that forest near your neck
Yet never so nex'
as to embrace this passion storm

The Washington Poems

Persecution

They tapped my phone and so I junked it.
They tapped my letters and so I burned them.
They tapped my knee and so I jerked it.

The Washington Poems

Analysts

Wits and pundits of the air
with their authoritative flair
Making opinions
facts pinioned
and points opined
the truth defined.

You have been covering the election beat
what will bring those victories sweet?
I say incumbency.
I say looks.
I say decency
the other guy's a crook.

After much study of the polls
there's a pattern which I've culled:
It shows a nation obsessed,
like its soaps, with success.
For in every district, great or small,
they've chosen a winner. That tells it all.
Whoever the candidates were that were run,
it's always been the winner who won.

But oh, our time has run its course.
Next week's another race and horse.

Pilgrim

When first we landed on these shores
We breathed a sigh for libertie
and said to tyranny, *Nevermore*
will we submit, or else we'll die.

Sweetheart

A sweetheart have you got?
I told him no, I've not
My heart is not sweet but bitter
bitter and badly broken

Imprisoned you are by desire
to make her servant of your fire

But she is so free and I so bound
this world whirling round
will when it hits the old refrain
find one less slave to sing it again

Extreme that is, whatever her beauty
To end it all for lust of body
or pain of heart or grief of soul
Is there nothing more past age of twenty

For a season only did I want
but now I have ceased
Ceased to want and ceased to care
for my life any

For just one pain
one loss of gain

Yet I was never stung or bited
as badly as by love unrequited
No, never so badly bit
as by love's unwanted respite

You have not seen the pain of age
Nor yet again its joys
These searing sorrows of the moment
are but a shallow wound
Deeper love will come with time
Just last until you see it
When life brings hope, the wisdom of years
reveals the folly of our fears

Romantic haste in drama brings
tears and sighs when the hero dies
but the curtain fall is final
when in life we take the tragic way
The sunset too is a glorious thing
but with it ends the day

Development

Under press of rents zoned very high
The mausoleate mansions of modernity
are raised to fill, not reach the skies
which had but humble homes heretofore
and churches, inns and stores

Parking for the life of nine to five
Widened streets, highways through the town
A world made for cars not men
Allowing no pedestrians

A remnant of a human time
about to make its exit from the scene
No matter if its beauty once was fine
or graced the drama, filled the art
of the years bygone
when style was not scorned
for office space in boxes unadorned

Overhead is seen
the menacing swing of the crane
surveying its property in the air
Clearing way for decade tiers
of honeycomb or tinted glass
monotony most crass
reflects no ghosts
of buildings lost, but fair
Still the beauty of the past

is not forgotten
The photographs and paintings
will recall
a world we can see but not reenter
Since developers, for renters, topple all

Yet even they will find a space
to mark the history of the place
Beside a vent or pipe
they will place their little plaque
if not in bronze, then in plastic:

On this site some time ago
an eyesore stood
but now, you can see
it is gone for good

The Washington Poems

Concession

What must not, What can not, has
The polls do not lie, alas
as much as we need for victory

The misery we await is not your fault
Your valiant fight History will exalt
and the voters blame for being inane

Yet further strife we must prevent
He may be Antichrist, but he's our President
And would surely say the same of me

So I use this last brief breath of fame
To leave you peace and grace and wisdom
And whatever else we lacked in our campaign.

Procession of Fall

Is not fall a magic time
when all the trees are set aflame
with oranges, reds and yellows
yet never by that fire consumed.

The mild winds blow and hug you
not too cold, not too hot
but softer afterthought
Of summer's heat

A calm for the mind
a balm for the heart
Ye have entered
the holy procession of Fall
Hear the trees shout their
Hallelujah colors
within the great grey walls
of the cathedral sky

Winter

The Washington Poems

Christmas

The town now has the crispness brought by cold
where all is firmest rock or vacant air
but for the powdered snow which, fold on fold,
upon each colored brick and iron stair
of houses laid like cookies in a row
prepares each street a festive treat for eyes;
and calls to mind the kindest overflow
of feasts and love attending our reprise
of when our Lord and Savior came to earth.
So giving to each other what we wish
we could have given Christ upon His birth.
Yet more He gives than we can lay on dish,
For which the angels' anthem can not cease:
All praise to God and to His people peace.

The Common Man

See the common man enthroned
not as man but as common
with average cruelty and mean spirit.
Can you not see?
Only a higher spirit raises man
from petty spites and fear
to spired worship of God.
When will this republic revere
that Holy Servant, Our Lord,
and humble itself to glory?

The Washington Poems

Laissez-faire

The rich man's silent war
waged against the poor.
All strings in his hand,
he says through his puppets:
We can not. give you more
than fair wages for the poor.

The Washington Poems

Prophetic Lament

All these consumed in bliss
their future doom presently miss
They blindly live, I a seer
But sight is naught but screams and tears
Away! Such thoughts will have their time
If time there be for them

Dispute

Where did you get that wallet, sir?
Don't slip it in your pack.
I don't want a thing that's yours;
I want my money back.
I need not be supplier, Pops,
for all the things you lack.
Now quick before I call the cops,
won't you return it, Mack?

The Washington Poems

Painting

Bodily pain I rarely notice
heartache fills my mind
Your absence is my greatest distress
I wilt without the sun

But present my pain is not the less
when I've your love not won
Yet win I must, for I die if I lose
In talent to trust, for you me to choose

Give me the brush and the painter's skill
on canvas to capture your beauty
Surely for this respect me you will
there is no more honorable duty

But this is too much, the task is such
as to make the imperfect falter
My gaudy oil would only spoil
and desecrate your altar

For if I studied a hundred years
with masterful hands in mine combined
and wrought an image in passion and tears
I could not fashion the beauty that I in you find

The Washington Poems

Sermon

Is it not enough that Christ our Lord died?
Should any other soul be crucified?
Accept His Passion as your punishment
Let His wounds your agony prevent
Then what self condemns, destroys,
Shall be claimed by mercy for joy.

Streets

When Time has quit its furious march
Through offices laid in infinite arch,
When adults have ceased to play in blocks,
From coffee's side the news it knocks
to settle as paper tents by glassy trunks

The herds of snorting cars
have stampeded to distant pasture
Leaving a prairie of parking lots
for a stray bison or Mustang to rot

Life has fled from town
Yet I, Death, live here
and all these live their deaths
the best they know not how
in this land of crowded loneliness.

Stalking the streets where lives bypass
Where all that glitters is broken glass
and beer cans and their tops and all
the accumulated waste of an ethylated existence

Death offers release, but I love my freedom.
I see you are dead to Death,
he says and leaves
turn and fall
then winter sets in
freezing many to life
their bodies cold as the pavement.

The Washington Poems

Home Ball

Athlete bearing his allegiance loudly
Playing to defend his hometeam's image
Redskins won in this game, so he proudly
Crashes home like Riggo through the scrimmage
Turning channels as the ballfields darken
Caught some B-ball in the ending minute
When the pace at last begins to quicken
Knowing this the final chance to win it
Pounding balls beat out the closing seconds
Matching baskets. *Miscues will destroy ya*
Bums miss passes, shots like that, he reckons
No, it's just a case of paran-Hoya
Satisfaction rooting for a winner
Cheers him as he eats a lonely dinner

The Washington Poems

The Prophet's Plea

Will you not listen and converse with God
If He is more than an abstract idea,
Why do you think that hearing Him is odd
and mock all those that think that they may see
a vision from the One who our sins bought,
who suffered and then died upon a cross
which was no dream, his pain no idle thought
No theory can redeem the sinner's loss
of righteousness and peace, but only Love
most Holy can restore us to the place
where we are wished to be by God, above
the sounds and sights of those untouched by grace,
To see the unseen, hear the unheard Word
and know the Truth: the glory of the Lord

The Washington Poems

Winterlight

White light on a snowy night
Brighter than I can catch in my weary sight.
Is this the gleam I see
When I dream of what to be?
Ever reaching for that star's height
Then it falls
as flakes upon me blow
the whispers of its glow
They say:
Yet still... it will
Yet still... it will

Festival of Peace

Is peace
a child's empty stomach
women living in the street
wealthy neglect of poor
in the quest for more
the anger of the masses
breeding young terror
old people kept from life
before they join the dead?

Is it the rule of despots
a knock in deadly night
It is needed
Oh, dare we say
it is needed here.
See the sweat of soul and substance
we gave to gain it.
It is needed, It is needed
The lusts of despots are always needed.

Is it the wall of tariffs
denying the poor the chance to sell?
Plump workers denying their slender cousins
escape from poverty's hell?

Is peace seen in vacant stares
despising sight of misery?
Or mocking eyes of soulless beauty
which can not stop their play to love?

Is it found in violent homes and streets,
where innocents are slaughtered
in the name of justice,
of right, or rights,
of everything but peace and light,
which knows the vicious error of hate?

Violence is its own injustice,
rarely stopping those who oppress.
The victim is victim twice
And murder only kills the harmless.

Now countless other miseries
come without a battle.
Cruelty does not await
the martial rattle.

How then do we say that peace has come
when wars alone have ceased?
Is it such a shallow thing,
not caring for the least?

Though all the guns be silenced,
each soldier in his home,
There is no peace till Love comes,
till the meek may safely roam.

Spring

The Washington Poems

Hymn

O Precious Savior
humbly at Thy cross I stand
pleading for mercy
freely given by Thine hand

Far have I travelled
Far into trouble, deep in strife
Peace yet is nearer
When in me You live Your life

The Washington Poems

Lincoln

A gangling giant rests with kindly gaze
upon the crowd which mills about his feet.
Could he but tell the trial of his days
to those who gather round his marble seat.
How viciously his public did malign
his fight to keep our people strong and free.
Yet this is just a statue in a shrine
of one whose words we do not hear, but see
on walls which scream no anguish, cry no tears
for gruesome battles bought with dad and son,
recall no blame he bore but, with the years,
forget the price at which ideals are won.
A hero now he can not move a knee.
The figure smiles at the irony.

Strolling Beauty

Beauty, know not your own beauty?
Nor loveliness, how you are loved?
You pass by a world of praises:
Our gift from heaven above,
cries the cardinal. The whippoorwill weeps,
Why, poor will be those that love her.
She can love but one in return.

More snares does she lay than are needed.
Rants the rabbit, *We will die in the trap*
and rot, our capture unheeded.
It is cruelty, she cares not.

From sleep, no rest can we wrest
nor take, claims the cat, *a nap.*
For stirred by her image, we yearn
and to slumber we never return.

And deep, the buck bays
is the pain in my heart.
Torn loose from it was a part
which leapt out as she bounded by.

The envious swan shows no grace
when to you she relinquishes her place.
But for her, my swains would be nigh.
Why? Why?

Yet Beauty hears none of these words.
What? Talking animals? Don't be absurd.
By a stream of tears, her eyes downcast,
She sighs, *Oh, do l have any charms?*
A million my love take me yet in your arms
And a hundred I'll tell you each day till my last.

Morning Knight

Back from the journeys
on the distant seas
in dreams of love and conquest
still fresh as is the air

Down the fields in glory
with giant strides advancing
Past ancient castle
the reddish stone hailing

A green rain of lime juice
hangs now from the trees
and upon the ground, the dew
raises grass to brighter hue

The pain of the battles
strikes him unawares
Yet his Savior sends a chill
to still the memory

It numbs my pain
O blest sobriety
My wounded heart
it alone maintains

Resumes the march with fresh resolve
and hope: *I am a nut*
But the Lord has blessed my words
to be the rustling of the leaves

Climbs up to the dome
once there he lifts his visor
The Crusader now is home
his counsel in the kingdom wiser

The Washington Poems

The King

The king dethroned
wears his crown
no more, no where
save in his proud and regal soul.

When captured, tortured, whipped and scourged,
That soul will stand
some more, some where
and still stand tall
and large and kind
against the common cruelty
of mankind.

Some hearts will be bitter
Some others be broken
are we not men?

Yet our souls are sound
to ring our coronation,
For this is our destiny:
To be kings again.

Stirring Dreams

To bound joyously towards
our great goal of peace
a peace mingled with prosperity
towards the sweetest pleasure
of trust and treasure
Yet more of love
of love proclaimed by loving all
Watering every flower
and feeding every soul
So all may grow
So all may grow

The Washington Poems

Wisdom

When men think me wise
I feel very foolish
Their measure ascribes
a wisdom to knowledge
But God is the rule
of true understanding

What then can I know
By searching with science
When my little thought
is fraught with errors

The Washington Poems

Artists

What is the unpaid worth
this labor in the dark?
Is poverty the just desert
of failing to mark
the profit before the gift?

The worker has his wages;
the investor his return.
They seek only the good which earns.
But for these your art is grown
who sow a pittance in ignorance
and reap what you make known.

What blame if you are paid a mite
It is no mete of merit
Though your stage is charity,
you are no parasite.
No fault of yours
but that of greedy souls
who give not freely of the purse
as you of your heart, your whole.

The Washington Poems

.

Mission

There is sweet longing for the mission alighted
Nervous joy of its early acquaintance
By the first touch of the work excited
The thrill growing in its moldings and shapings
Then ecstasy when entered wholly in the task

Next blissful care, the project nourished
Soon swelling achievement in life
But in pain is born the mission accomplished
For nothing is made glorious
but by laborious strife

Renwick

Have you gone to see
Grandma Gallery
Slept in her velvet chairs
in the rooms upstairs
Dreamt of life within the frame
or played some other game
of mind upon the walls
or walking through her halls
What treasured scenes did Grandma store
on her cozy second floor
What treasures more we'd find, and magic
if she but let us in her attic

The Washington Poems

Corinthians Reading

The streams of tinted light
over wooden pews
Gave peace, assent, delight
by its flood in hues

The words assuring
ushered in
a well of hope upspringing

For now we see but dimly
as if through a clouded glass
But then most clearly shall we
see Thee face to face.

In part we see, in part we know,
but then in full both see and know
as we are fully known.

The Washington Poems

A Child Speaks

A bud I am
Yet caught in weeds
Needing soil and water
my roots to feed
And guiding light from sun above,
To rise up to the break of day
And cheer each creature on his way.
For when the warmth of heavenly grace
Shines upon this shying bud,
In a smile of petals, it opens its face
And shares with all its beauty and love.

www.ingramcontent.com/pod-product-compliance
Lightning Source LLC
LaVergne TN
LVHW041302080426
835510LV00009B/841